CW01583040

My Prayer Book

by
Graham Jeffery

Dear Lord
I am a little child
in the morning
of my life
And I know
that you will stay with me
till evening comes.

© Copyright 1993 by Kevin Mayhew Ltd.

KEVIN MAYHEW LTD
Rattlesden Bury St Edmunds
Suffolk England
IP30 0SZ

Lutheran Publishing House
205 Halifax Street
Adelaide
SA 5000
Australia

ISBN 0 86209 446 1

Printed in Great Britain

Early in the morning I will love you.

This is the day the Lord has made.

I will rejoice and be glad.

How shall I sing the Lord's song?

Wash me and I shall be clean.

The Lord himself is my helper.
He stands beside me when I'm afraid.

Man goes out to his labour
until the evening.

You lead me by the hand.

You show me the way that I should go.

Your hands have made me,
and loved me.

You are the strength of my life.

High and low, rich and poor,
one with another.

You are everyone's friend.

You run to help me when
I'm in trouble.

You mend what is broken
and make it better.

When my friends forget me,
you come to visit me.

Your love holds me up.

You are my shade in the heat.

You are my shelter in the rain.

You are with me all the days
of my life.

Your love reaches me everywhere.

Take me out of the muddy pit –
out of the mud and clay.

I will rest by still waters.

You lead me to my journey's end.

You prepare a table for me.

You are my light in the darkest place.

I will lie down in peace
and take my rest.

It is only you, Lord,
who make me live in safety.

You make
my darkness
to be light.